I0081010

LEARN

PROACTIVE
PARENTING

DO

TEACH

PROACTIVE PARENTING
Copyright © 2016

Unless otherwise noted, all scripture taken from
THE HOLY BIBLE, NEW INTERNATIONAL VERSION®,
NIV® Copyright © 1973, 1978, 1984, 2011 by Biblica, Inc.™
Used by permission. All rights reserved worldwide.

ISBN-13: 978-1-935256-55-7

Ledge Press
PO Box 1652
Boone, NC 28607
www.ledgepress.com
ledgepress@gmail.com

TABLE OF CONTENTS

INTRODUCTION

Today, there are more resources and programs focused on teaching God's inherent Truth than ever before. Churches have access to an enormous amount of Bible study materials from wellknown and qualified theologians. Pastors, leaders, and teachers have the ability to find an almost unlimited supply of curriculum designed specifically to lead people to a deeper walk in their journey with the Lord. The church, now more than ever, is very well-equipped with the resources they need to make disciples.

With that said, Steve Wright in his book *ReThink* stated, "The church must excel in instructing and equipping moms and dads in all aspects of family life, especially discipling their children." Therefore, the church has the responsibility to provide discipleship opportunities for the entire family with excellence. When the church strives to do this, they are fulfilling God's command, "Go and make disciples" (Matt. 28:19a).

I will be the first to say that pastors, leaders, and teachers are commanded by the Lord to offer discipleship opportunities with quality and excellence. It is time for us to roll up our sleeves and get to work equipping "people for works of service, so that the body of Christ may be built up" (Ephesians 4:12). Discipleship will cost us everything we've got, but it will be the greatest investment of our ministries. So pastors, leaders, and teachers...let's get to work!

However, the door swings both ways. Moms and dads need to take advantage of the church's discipleship offerings and get fully engaged. Parents should strategically and purposefully integrate their family into a local church that stands on solid Biblical teaching and offers quality discipleship opportunities.

How connected are parents with what your church offers regarding discipleship? Parents today have the chance to engage in small groups, discipleship groups, mentoring, and prayer groups to become growing disciples. However, there is a sad reality. Many parents have used the church not so much for their own spiritual edification but as a place to drop off their kids so the paid professionals can provide Biblical education for their children. Many parents are not engaging, and this lack of teamwork has to end. The church and the home need to come together, work together, and even pull together as one. When both institutions are unified, they will be able to accomplish extraordinary things.

Two old farmers entered their horses in a horse pull competition. The object of the contest was to hitch the animal to a weighted sled and have the horse attempt to pull the sled a certain distance. The first farmer's horse won first place by pulling a 700-pound sled. The other farmer's horse finished second. The runner-up horse was only able to pull a 500-pound sled.

After the contest the two farmers decided to hitch both horses together to see just how much weight they could pull together. Many people assumed that the two animals would pull 1,200 pounds. To everyone's amazement both horses together pulled the 1,200-pound sled with ease. They didn't stop there. The horses pulled 1,400, 1,600, even an 1,800-pound sled. The farmers kept adding weight to the sled and the two horses together were able to astonish the crowd by pulling 1,900 pounds. This is an awesome illustration of the importance of teamwork. God has designed the church and the home to come together as a team when it comes to discipleship. The church is commanded to provide the equipping, and the parents are commanded to be the primary disciplers of their children. When the two come together, God can do some incredible things in the life of the family.

I believe the church and the home have the potential to be the most viable and influential institutions for discipling kids when both work together as a team...and our culture needs it now more than ever! That's why I bring you this book. It's my goal to help you see God's command to parents to be learners of the Bible, doers of His commands, and teachers of Scripture to their children. In other words, I want to help you teach the parents of your congregation how to become **Proactive Parents.**

CHAPTER 1
LEARN, DO, TEACH

*…equip God's people to do his work and build up
the church.*
Ephesians 4:12 NLT

At a Christian conference, I had the opportunity to speak to several church leaders about family ministry. During the meeting I played a game called, "Do you remember when…?" I asked the group questions like, "Do you remember when all you had in your house was a black and white TV?" "Do you remember when five dollars was enough to be considered gas money?" "Do you remember when stores closed on Saturday night not to reopen until Monday morning?"

These questions quickly divided the room into two distinct groups. The first group, who was around fifty years old and older, sat back in their seats and let their thoughts walk down memory lane. Their minds were flooded with fond memories recalling what life was like in their childhood homes. They reflected on heart-warming times of days gone by. While the first group was steeped in nostalgia, the other group was sitting up in their seats in disbelief thinking, "What are these people doing? How could there have been anything good about those old days?"

Eventually the younger group in the room came to the realization that their counterparts were not aliens. They began to see that there were many more benefits to those old days than they first realized. My purpose for playing this game was actually strategic. I wanted to get people to think about the vast differences of our culture today versus what life was like just a few short decades ago. At that point I made a slight transition in the game.

While the entire group was hanging in the moment, I began to ask a series of questions pertaining to issues Christians have encountered over the last forty to fifty years. I asked, "Do you remember when all the couples living in your neighborhood were married instead of just living together? Do you remember when you heard for the first time that someone you knew was homosexual? Do you remember when there was never a thought of gay couples getting married?" These were only a few of the questions I asked to get the crowd thinking about how our society has deteriorated over the years. As you may have guessed, my goal was to bring into focus the collapse of Biblical principles and to expose the lack of Christian influence in our homes.

This game has proven to be a great tool to get people of all generations to think about the environment in which the current generation is growing up. As we stand back and look at the panoramic view of today's cultural landscape, we find ourselves asking an important question. What have been the contributing factors to get us in the mess we're in today? Unfortunately there are no easy answers to this difficult question. However, it does lead us into a healthy evaluation process.

There are many variables that can be linked to our cultural demise, but there are two prominent elements that begin to surface. Of a long list of contributors, our sex-crazed culture easily lands somewhere near the top. However, the other major factor to our cultural tailspin may come as a surprise. The tension that exists between the church and the home has also proven to be an unexpected contributor to this problematic trend.

When asked to complete this well known advertising phrase "sex _____," what is the first thing that comes to your mind? My guess would be that you responded by saying: "sells." We live in a sex-crazed culture where sexual images are coming at us from every direction. Movies, television, publications, and the music industry are relentlessly pounding our culture with risqué dress, provocative pictures, and tantalizing lyrics. It should come as no surprise to parents that children, especially teens, are targeted by these industries. Their minds are constantly bombarded with a myriad of false ideas. They constantly hear lies like: "Have sex anywhere, with anyone, whenever you can." "You are the authority. No one tells you what to do." "You need to dress like this celebrity if you want to be cool."

It doesn't stop there. Many of today's iconic performers show little to no regard for morals or modesty. They will say and do anything if it means they can maintain their popularity in the public eye. In other words, they will do whatever it takes to stay popular. Unfortunately, in many cases today that means the new up-and-coming pop-stars have to be more X-rated to outdo their predecessors. Sadly, these ideologies are accepted, embraced, and in many ways imitated by many kids and teens in our culture.

Another cause for our culture's downfall can be attributed to the tension that lies between the church and the home. From pastors' perspectives there is nothing they want to see more than every child and student in their ministries following the Lord and grow-

Church & Home Tension
A. Surrendered to Christ
B. Sports Star
C. GPA & SAT
D. Popularity

ing deeper in their relationships with Christ. Pastors know and understand that sports, grades, and popularity with peers are important parts of a young person's life. But hands down, making Jesus the absolute Lord of their lives is at the top of the list. Nothing should rival having God at the forefront of anyone's life. There is no surprise that parents are quick to stack their hands on top of their pastor's hand and say that they too want nothing more than for their kids to believe in Christ, be a light in a dark world, and spend their lives serving the Lord.

But here is where the tension comes into play. Many parents will have a Jesus plus _____ (fill in the blank) mentality when it comes to their children's lives outside of church. Their words say, "I want my kids to get saved and live for Jesus" but their actions suggest "now that you're saved, we can concentrate on other important things."

For instance, parents want their kids to get saved but they will over encourage their children to participate in sports with the assumption that their little athlete will receive a scholarship to pay their way through college. More times than not, playing sports fills a family's calendar leaving little room for church activities. Other parents want their children serving the Lord but they push their kids to make straight A's to give them an added edge on their high school transcripts. Students can easily feel pressure to put in long hours of study to make the higher grades giving them no room or energy for personal discipleship. Moms and dads want their children to be surrendered followers of Christ and evangelize the lost. However, many are afraid of their children not being socially accepted. They will strongly insist that their kids attend all the popular gatherings, wear the newest fashion, and stay up-to-date with the latest gadget. When a home emphasizes these priorities, it has the potential of conveying the materialistic attitude, "We have to keep up with the Joneses."

To be fair, there is nothing wrong with being a sports star and excelling in athletics. Sports teach teamwork and promote physical health. The same is true with school. There is nothing wrong with making good grades and working hard to achieve academic excellence. God is delighted when we desire to learn about all He has created. In the same way, having a lot of friends and being popular in social circles is wonderful. The Lord has made us for fellowship.

Looking back at the Church and Home Tension list, points B through D can give a surrendered follower of Christ many great opportunities to share his faith and be a light to others who do not have a personal relationship with Jesus. But when moms and dads place greater priority on the portion of the list that has no eternal significance it sends a contradicting message. On the one hand, children who have put their faith in Christ hear the church saying, "God is first and everything else is second." But on the other hand, their parents are constantly elevating a lifestyle that is focused on temporal things. In the end, children and students are pulled in two different directions which can easily lead to confusion. As a result, tension is created between the church and the home.

In my twenty plus years of student ministry I've seen first hand what happens when parents allow this sex-crazed culture to penetrate their home. A child can form the wrong ideas about themselves and other people. I have also watched parents persistently push their kids too hard in the non-eternal directions. Children can develop a poor perspective about the material things God has placed in this world. When moms and dads allow either or both of these prominent cultural elements to enter their homes, the children are the ones who ultimately suffer. This is a problem.

The good thing is solving problems is what the Bible does best. That truth never ceases to amaze me. But what really blows me away is the fact that scripture, written thousands of years ago, actually speaks about this exact same problem. In the book of Deuteronomy, Moses is giving the children of Israel some final reminders and instructions before entering into the Promised Land. The one hundred twenty year old prophet gives them some important information regarding their obedience to God's commands. He makes it crystal clear that their continued prosperity and their family's future blessing in the new land hinges on the nation's compliance to God's requirements. The reason Moses gives the Israelite nation this counsel is simple. He knew about the pagan people who occupied the land of promise and the wicked idols they worshiped.

When you study the Old Testament and learn about the gods the Canaanite nations worshiped you find two prominent idols among their pantheon of deities…. Asherah and Baal. Asherah was known as the fertility or sex goddess while Baal was the prosperity or materialism god (a.k.a. god of temporal things). When you take these two gods and compare them to the issues we face in our culture today, you find eerie similarities. Our families are confronted with the same idols the Jews encountered. The only difference is we no longer call them Asherah and Baal. We call them lust and greed. Moses wasn't only speaking to the Israelites in the book of Deuteronomy; he is also whispering into our ears today. God's Word says as much to us now as it did back then. Funny how timeless and relevant the Bible is.

When we step back and try to piece together our discussion to this point, we come to a disturbing conclusion. The sex-crazed, materialistic culture seems to be plummeting more and more out of control. Our children and homes are under an enormous attack. With gender confusion now becoming more of an issue and with the legalizing of marijuana in the US, many Christians sit in bewilderment and ask, "What could possibly be next?"

This question is difficult to answer because it only generates more questions. For instance, will a forty year old man be able to marry a twelve year old girl one day in this country? Will a thirtyfive year old woman be able to lawfully wed her dog? It's hard to tell since the next thing is so tightly tied to our depraved nature.

With the growing darkness overshadowing our world, many Christians feel hopeless. Christ followers desperately want to know the answer to this most pressing question but are almost afraid to ask, "Is there any hope for our children and grandchildren?" Even in our growing anti-Christian culture I will be the first to answer with a resounding, "Yes!" There is hope! How do I know this? Simple. God the Father is in heaven on His throne and His Son, Jesus, is seated at His right side. As long as the Godhead is in place there is always hope...

hope for our culture, hope for our children, hope for our homes. But where do we begin, and does God have an answer?

It starts with humility. The Bible says, "Humble yourselves before the Lord, and he will lift you up" (James 4:10). We have to acknowledge to the Lord that we have been unfaithful to Him by committing the many sins related to false gods like Asherah, Baal, and others. Once we have sought repentance and turned our hearts back to Him, it becomes easy to find the answer to this complicated problem. Fortunately, we don't have to look any further than back to the instructions Moses gave to the Children of Israel.

Israel, God's chosen people, were faced with an ominous task. The nations who occupied the Land of Promise were no pushovers. There were "seven nations larger and stronger" (Deuteronomy 7:1) than the forty-year, desert-dwelling nomads. But they were no match for the Lord of Hosts. God had a plan to rid the land of the pagans and make good on His word to their forefathers-Abraham, Isaac, and Jacob. Moses explains to the Israelites that the Lord would be the One who "drives out before you many nations…" (Deuteronomy 7:1) and it would be their job to "destroy them totally" (Deuteronomy 7:2) and "break down their altars, smash their sacred stones, cut down their Asherah poles" (Deuteronomy 7:5). The Lord's plan to conquer the land would give His people houses they didn't build, wells they didn't dig, vineyards they didn't plant, and the opportunity to begin a new life. But this was only part of His overall strategy. God would also instruct Moses to share with the Israeli parents and grandparents His blueprint of how to grow and thrive in the Promised Land now and for generations to come.

Moses said to Israel, "Now, Israel, hear the decrees and laws I am about to teach you. Follow them so that you may live and may go in and take possession of the land the LORD, the God of your ancestors, is giving you… Only be careful, and watch yourselves closely so that you do not forget the things your eyes have seen or let them fade from your heart as long as you live. Teach them to your children and to their children after them" (Deuteronomy 4:1,9).

When we break down these two verses we clearly see the Lord has three things in mind. God tells leaders of each home to be eager learners of His Word, authentic doers of His Word, and genuine teachers of His Word. In short God is saying, "Make disciples."

Notice the Bible says, "hear the decrees and laws I am about to teach you." When Moses uses the word teach he is naturally implying that his audience are learners. (Learn) As he continues, scripture says, "Follow them." Moses instructs them next to not just be hearers of the Word but to also be doers of the Word. (Learn - Do) The end of verse nine combines the efforts of the learner and doer of God's Word into a practical conclusion. The Bible says, "Teach them to your children and to their children after them." Unapologetically, the Lord narrows his audience to a specific group of people. To make sure there is no confusion, God gives the teaching responsibility of His laws and commands to the parents and grandparents. (Learn – Do – Teach) Why does He do this? It is simple. There is no group of people better suited to share the Lord's instructions with the next generation. Parents and grandparents are not only commanded to pass their faith down to their children, but they also have the most time and influence in their young lives to be able to do so.

The Lord set up the Israelites then and equips His followers today in a perfect yet simplistic way. Putting into action the Learn – Do – Teach methodology gives the next generation the greatest chance to be prosperous and successful. It takes determination to be a real learner. It takes an uncompromising attitude to be a sincere doer. It takes total and complete surrender to be a teacher your kids and grandkids need for the world they are encountering. As good as that is, here's the best part. God doesn't just tell us to implement the Learn – Do – Teach strategy in our homes and then leave us hanging to do it the best we can. The Lord gives us detailed instructions in His Word on how to accomplish this arduous task. As we will see in the remaining chapters, God reveals to us easy ways to incorporate disciple-making into the rhythm of our lives so that it can become a natural part of our homes.

Question for the Pastor, Leader, Teacher reading this book: Do the people in your congregation lack focus, conviction, and stamina when it comes to disciplines of the faith, disciplines such as in-depth study of the Bible, living a life of holiness and integrity, and discipling others based on God's standards? Read on and let's explore together what God's Word has to say about empowering believers to become the disciples the Lord has designed them to be: the disciple-makers the following generations need, and hope for the future.

CHAPTER 2
LEARN

"…you shall learn them and be careful to do them."
Deuteronomy 5:1b ESV

Brian Herbert once said, "The capacity to learn is a gift, the ability to learn is a skill, the willingness to learn is a choice." Learning is essential in life. That's why the Bible gives the simple command to "learn" God's commands and "follow them" multiple times in the book of Deuteronomy (4:1,10, 5:1, 6:1, 8:1, 11:1). Jesus gives the same simple command in Matthew 11:29 when He says, "…take up My yoke and learn from Me…" Paul tells us "For whatever was written in the past was written for our instruction, so that we may have hope through endurance and through the encouragement from the Scriptures" (Romans 15:4). "Let the word of Christ dwell in you richly in all wisdom, teaching and admonishing one another…" (Colossians 3:16 NKJV). Peter also gives us the same simple instruction when he says, "So we have the prophetic Word strongly confirmed. You will do well to pay attention to it…" 2 Peter 1:19. John gives us reassurance when he says, "For this is what love for God is: to keep His commands. Now His commands are not a burden…" (1 John 5:3).

Each of these verses have one important thing in common. The Lord expects His followers to read His Word (learn) and do what it says. The days of the prophets are gone. It's been about two thousand years since Jesus walked the earth. Paul, Peter, John, and the other disciples have all passed away. But Peter mentioned, "…we have the prophetic Word." The Lord has made sure we can have His infallible Word, His personal revelation, His instruction for life in our possession…"so that we may have hope." Jesus also mentions, "…the Advocate, the Holy Spirit, whom the Father will send in my name, will teach you all things and will remind you of everything I have said to you" (John 14:26). God has seen to it that we have the Bible plus His Holy Spirit. What more do we need? That's why He doesn't hold back when He tells us to "learn" and "follow" His commands.

The Bible not only gives us the simple command to learn, it also provides excellent examples of people who loved learning. All those who gathered near Capernaum to hear Jesus preach were astounded by His message. The Bible says, "When Jesus had finished this sermon, the crowds were astonished at His teaching, because He was teaching them like one who had authority, and not like their scribes" (Matthew 7:28-29). Also, as the church was in it's beginning stages, scripture tells us the believers, "…devoted themselves to the apostles' teaching, to the fellowship, to the breaking of bread, and to the prayers" (Acts 2:42).

Perhaps one of the greatest examples of authentic learning is displayed by a woman named Mary. During

His ministry, Jesus traveled throughout Galilee. One day He came to a small town named Bethany. The Bible says, "He entered a village, and a woman named Martha welcomed Him into her home. She had a sister named Mary, who also sat at the Lord's feet and was listening to what He said" (Luke 10:38-39). Mary found no greater place to be than sitting at the feet of Jesus as He taught. Her entire attention was riveted on their honored guest. There was nothing that would distract her from consuming every word that came off the lips of her Lord. Mary was captivated. Why? She loved Jesus. As a result of that love, her priority was to listen to Christ's words for the sole purpose of allowing them to rule her thoughts, actions, attitude, speech, etc... (Luke 11:28) Mary beautifully modeled the attitude of a genuine learner.

How awesome would it be to have churches in North America filled with learners like we see in scripture... people who are "astonished by Christ's teaching"...parents who "devote themselves to the teaching of God's Word" and want to "sit at the feet of Jesus." God wants moms and dads who intently want to study the scriptures, listen to quality Bible teaching, seek to hear the Lord speak to them through prayer, and authentically do what He says. Wouldn't it be great to see parents leading their families this way?

For this to occur, there must be a priority shift in parents' lives. The Bible makes it clear that born again believers in Jesus Christ we are to be learners of scripture. To be a learner of the Word, a person has to be a reader of the Word. To be a reader of the Word, one has to make reading the Word his priority. When the Word is a believer's priority he, like Mary, will be captivated by the Savior and want to be imitators of Him (Ephesians 5:1). Why? Because he loves Jesus and wants to be obedient to Him.

Is this happening in our churches? For many moms and dads it is. They are in the Word daily and striving to live out God's commands each day through the power of the Holy Spirit. Their desire is to be great learners and authentic doers of His Word. They are on fire. As exciting as that is, the sad reality is the percentage of parents who are in that group is small and seemingly decreasing in size. Thus a second group emerges who have a plethora of shallow rationalizations for why they do not make learning God's Word a priority.

Is this really a problem? Should there be any concern? When we read books, articles, and reports from reputable organizations like The Barna Group, George Gallup, and The Pew Report we get choked by all their data and percentages. Regrettably, there is a disappointing common thread found in all their research. America is Biblically illiterate. As a matter of fact, it could be said the North American church has become Biblically anemic...perhaps anorexic. Many Christians are not searching the Scripture for its deep, life-giving Truths. There is little to no time spent digging into God's Word to know Him more intimately. By in large, the people who fill our pews Sunday after Sunday have Bibles they do not read and consequently do not obey. Therefore, those who call themselves believers in Jesus Christ lack power, vitality, and are overall weak in their faith. Here's a thought, perhaps it's time to remove the man caves and replace them with studies instead.

As often as I can, I like to talk to parents and ask them questions about their Bible knowledge, their theology, and scriptural facts. I try to use my conversation to maneuver to the question I really want to ask which is: "How's your daily time with the Lord?" For the "on fire" group they always have something good to say. But it's a different story for those in the "non-on fire" or "stagnant" group. I hear a wide variety of reasons, excuses, and confessions as to why their intimacy with the Lord is so lacking. For some people, time is the big issue. They are too busy with family or their job, therefore Bible reading gets postponed or squeezed out all together. Others complain that scripture is not relevant in today's world (Hebrews 4:12-13) so they spend little to no time in the Word. Some will only read depthless devotionals or selective portions because they see the Bible as too confrontational to their preferred way of life (2 Timothy 3:16). There are those who neglect reading scripture all together for the simple fact they are not disciplined (1 Timothy 4:7-8). Then there are others who try to justify their lack of daily Bible reading from the standpoint that scripture is too hard to understand (John 8:43, 1 Corinthians 2:14). Needless to say, this is not an exhaustive list of excuses given by parents who fight against learning God's Word. This leads to the question: "Are parents letting the Word dwell in them richly" (Colossians 3:16)? I'd say not enough. We definitely have a problem.

Why do we have a growing number of parents in this "stagnant" group? There are numerous answers that could be given. For instance, "Things are going so well in America that Christians have dropped their guard." "Pastors are setting the bar too low by preaching feel good, Christianity lite messages from their pulpits." Or "Parents think salvation is enough so putting forth the effort to be a learner of God's Word is not necessary." All these and more are plausible causes. However, there is one common denominator that lies underneath our current situation that is actually the culprit...Parents are not in love with Jesus. The evidence is seen in a single New Testament quote by the Lord. He said, "If you love me, keep my commands" (John 14:15). It's important to consider the verb tense of "keep." It is in the imperative mood. This means the word is an absolute command. No ifs, ands, or buts. Simply put, the Bible says it so you do it. That's true love. That's true obedience.

What does complete obedience look like in parents' lives today? It looks like Mary's life. It's moms and dads being fed and challenged by great Bible teachers. They want nothing other than to be taught the Word of God. Complete obedience is seen when parents hear Jesus say, "...take up My yoke and learn (imperative mood) from Me..." (Matthew 11:29), and it fuels their desire to dig deep into the scriptures. Their study increases their knowledge of the Word and empowers them to authentically live out God's commands. Completely obedient parents are Christians who faithfully allow the Word to dwell (imperative mood) in them richly (Colossians

3:16). They let nothing distract them from intentionally letting the Word live in them abundantly every day. If moms and dads would surrender their lives and become completely obedient to the Lord, homes in our culture would transform. Being a learner of God's commands would be the way of life (John 14:21, 23,) and the "stagnant" group would cease to exist.

When parents truly love Jesus and His Word and, as a result, want to obey scripture, something extraordinary has the potential of taking place in their homes. Moms and dads can be an integral part of their family's growing faith. Not only that, they can also lay a solid God-centered foundation for future generations. However, there is one piece of the puzzle the Bible says is still remaining. Ephesians 5:18 says, "Do not get drunk on wine, which leads to debauchery. Instead, be filled with the Spirit." Without the filling of the Holy Spirit, parents do not have the ability to love Jesus properly, understand scripture adequately, or obey God's Word sufficiently.

Next to the new birth there is nothing more important for Christian parents than to understand the infilling of the Holy Spirit. How can moms and dads in today's culture be filled? There are three important truths to consider from my mentor Dr. Bill Bennett:

The filling of the Holy Spirit is a command.

In Ephesians 5:18 "be filled with the Spirit" answers this question. This command is in the imperative mood. It isn't optional. Every believer is commanded to be filled and controlled by the Spirit. The command is plural which means that the command is given to all of us – not just to "super saints" or "spiritual giants." The command is in the passive voice. This means we don't fill ourselves. The filling comes from an outside source – the Holy Spirit. The command is in the present tense. This means the filling is a repeated event. This truth should make us shake in our boots! It should make the foundations of our souls tremble with fear that not to be filled with the Holy Spirit is a grievous sin.

The filling of the Holy Spirit takes great effort.

Desire to be filled. Being filled begins with desire. As a good football coach tells his embattled troops at half-time, "Guys, you gotta want to." Jesus said "If anyone thirst or hunger, he will be filled." (Matthew 5:6; John 7:37). "Does this describe you? Are you thirsty – maybe a little desperate – for a closer walk with God? Do you ever find yourself crying out with the psalmist? 'My soul thirsts for God, for the living God. When can I go and meet with God?' (Psalm 42:2). Jesus said that when the Holy Spirit controls you, you will have a hunger and a thirst to know God and grow in Him. Out of this acute, life- defining thirst comes the Spirit-controlled life.

Denounce all the known sin in your life. Confession of sin is critical, but denunciation is a step beyond confession. I might confess to a problem with impure thoughts, but what good does that do if I go out and buy a Playboy magazine this afternoon? Paul says,

"Since we have these promises, dear friends, let us purify ourselves from everything that contaminates body and spirit, perfecting holiness out of reverence for God" (2 Corinthians 7:1).

When we come to be filled with the Spirit, we have to cleanse our hearts through the shed blood of the Lord Jesus Christ. We have to say, 'God, if there is any sin in my life, if there's something I'm doing that isn't pleasing to You, put Your finger on it. Parents need to say to the Lord, "Search me, God, and know my heart; test me and know my anxious thoughts. See if there is any offensive way in me…" (Ps 139:23-24). In other words, show me where my sins are Lord and I will denounce them. I will confess them, and I will turn from them.

You can't be filled with the Holy Spirit while you're harboring your own little pet sins. Maybe it's a place to which you go, a relationship in which you're involved, the types of entertainment you indulge in, or a habit you've clung to for years – something that you know violates God's standards. You will never be filled with the Spirit of God until you denounce it, confess it, and forsake it. The Holy Spirit isn't just a title. That's who He is, and He doesn't enjoy living in an unclean environment. If there is known, unconfessed sin in your life, the Holy Spirit will not take control. The very fact of your sin is evidence that He isn't in control."

Die to self (2 Corinthians 4:10). To be filled with the Spirit is to yield to His control. It is to take self off the throne of your heart and enthrone Jesus. Romans 12:1-2 are absolute keys to the Spirit-controlled life.

Depend fully upon the Holy Spirit. A better word is surrender. Surrender is just the opposite of rededication of life or what we call commitment. When we commit to the Lord, we name the terms of our commitment. When we surrender, we let Him set the terms.

The filling of the Holy Spirit requires surrender.

The infilling of the Holy Spirit is the control of the Holy Spirit over the believer's life and occurs when one surrenders his life completely to the control of the Holy Spirit. Luke 5:26 states that the disciples were "filled" with fear, meaning they were controlled or dominated by the emotion of fear. The word "filled" in Luke 5:26 is the same word found in Ephesians 5:18, "Be filled with the Spirit." While the baptism of the Holy Spirit occurs only once, the infilling may occur at a crisis moment, but it continually occurs as one surrenders to the Holy Spirit. Can one lose the infilling? Indeed he can and often does.[1]

What would a Spirit filled, God loving, Bible learning, obedient parent look like? They would be constantly motivated to be a student of the Bible. Their prayer would be powerful. Their testimony would be pure. Sincerity would be in their worship. Their words would be uplifting.

Hope and joy would fill their hearts. Thanksgiving would be on their lips. Their integrity would be obvious. Parents would seek unity with others and love sacrificially.

---

[1] Bill Bennett, *Mentoring Men for the Master 1.1*, (L'Edge Press, 2012), 22-26.

Would there be any difference in Spirit filled homes? Without a doubt, God's Word would be priority. Disciple-making would be in the hands of the parents. Forgiveness of wrongs would abound. Grace would trump guilt. Mercy would reign. Peace would rule. Families would experience patience during affliction. Imitation of Christ would be their goal. Holiness would be the family standard. Children would be surrendered followers of Christ. Basically, Spirit-filled homes would exude power and vitality in this and future generations.

Question for the Pastor, Leader, Teacher reading this book: Spirit filled families are the homes I hope for. Now the tough question is, "Are you encouraging parents to do whatever it takes to be filled with the Holy Spirit so they can be learners of the very words He inspired?" Every generation will be beneficiaries.

CHAPTER 3
DO

"...you shall learn them and be careful to do them."
Deuteronomy 5:1b ESV

Undeniably, Michael Jordan was the greatest NBA player during the late 1980's and 1990's. With a lifetime average of 30.1 points and 5.3 assists per contest, his six championship rings prove MJ was a dominant force on the court. However, an interesting bit of trivia that is hard not to notice is that during his illustrious basketball career he was never the highest paid player in the NBA. When asked why he never held out on his contract to force the Chicago Bulls to pay him more money Jordan replied, "I have always honored my word. I went for security. I had sixyear contracts, and I always honored them. People said I was underpaid, but when I signed on the dotted line, I gave my word." After his career, several high profile players demanded contract renegotiations. A reporter asked Jordan if he were still in the game would he stand on his previous decision. Michael quickly stated, "What if my kids saw their dad breaking a promise? How could I continue training them to keep their word?" He went on to say,

"You stand by your word, even when that might go against you."

Whenever I hear stories like this I cannot help to connect them to people of the Bible. People in the Old Testament like Joseph, Moses, Hannah, Daniel, and others in the New Testament like Mary, Joseph, Paul, and, of course, Jesus were all known for their integrity. Scripture is not only full of people with integrity but saturated with commands for believers to live a pure and blameless life. One passage that stands out most is found in Philippians 1:9-10. Paul challenges the church at Philippi with the importance of personal and relational integrity. He prayed, "And this is my prayer: that your love may abound more and more in *knowledge* and *depth of insight*, so that you may be able to *discern* what is best and may be *pure* and *blameless* for the day of Christ."

There are several words in these verses that need a closer look. Notice how Paul says in verse nine that he is praying for the believers' love to abound in knowledge. The word he uses for knowledge (epignōsis) means to have a deep, advanced understanding of scripture. It is a keen grasp of scripture that can only occur when a follower diligently studies (learns) the Bible.

He then mentions he is praying for their depth of insight (aisthēsis). This word refers to the understanding given to believers by the Holy Spirit to rightly apply God's Truth in their lives. It means followers have the supernatural ability to comprehend biblical, moral, and spiritual concepts. In other words, they have the mind of Christ (1 Corinthians 2:16).

Paul goes even deeper as he uses a simple transitional phrase "so that" to move from knowledge and insight to the word discern in verse ten. Discern (dokimazō) implies that Christ's followers examine, investigate, and study the best ways to obey and please the Lord (Ephesians 5:10) in all they do (1 Corinthians 10:31). Because of their great love for Christ, believers desire to live at only the highest spiritual levels of maturity. With all their hearts, they are no longer just committed to the Lord but surrendered to Him. Their faith is growing stronger not weaker. There is such a transformation in their lives, they base their actions, thoughts, attitudes, etc…on God's Word not the whims of their old way of life.

At this point, Paul has set the stage to reveal how this knowledge, insight, and discernment are played out in a believer's life. He begins with the word pure. "Pure" (eilikrinēs) has two possible meanings according to blueletterbible.org. It means, "1- Pure, Sincere, Unsullied. 2 - Found pure when unfolded and examined by the sun's light." Another definition describes pure to mean "without wax."

In ancient Rome fine pottery was hard to manufacture, thus making it an expensive commodity. For instance, skilled pottery merchants would turn clay on a wheel to shape it into a thin, lightweight, round plate. When the potter was satisfied with his work, it would be kiln dried until cured. Once the firing process was complete, the unblemished finished product would bring the potter a sizable profit. However, there was always the risk of thin pottery developing cracks as it cured. Potters with integrity would simply discard the fractured products and begin again. On the other hand, the more unscrupulous potters would fill the cracks with hard, dark wax to hide the flaws of the piece. Once the plate was glazed or painted the imperfections were concealed and sold as perfect merchandise.

Wise buyers were always cautious when purchasing pottery. They knew to inspect a dealer's product before buying. The customer would hold the plate up toward the sun to allow light rays to shine through the pottery. If they were able see dark streaks in the piece, they knew the merchant had most likely filled the cracks with wax to cover up defects. This became such a common practice that integrity-minded sellers would stamp their pottery with the Latin words sine cera (without wax) as a guarantee of high quality. Scripture here is plainly saying that believers should have a sine cera (without wax) inward lifestyle.

Even though our lives are filled with cracks, the Lord urges believers to aspire to live with an inward integrity at all costs. Of course this idea has a direct connection to John 14:15 where Jesus says, "If you love me, keep my commands." A "wax-less" Christian, even though covered with many flaws, will strive with all his heart to honor the Lord by obeying His commands. His love for Christ compels him to surrender his thoughts, attitudes, desires, and all other inward characteristics to live in ways that please (Ephesians 5:10) his Savior.

Paul strategically couples the word "blameless" (aproskopos) with the word "pure" for an important reason. Pure carries the idea of an inward integrity while blameless conveys outward integrity. Blameless, as defined by blueletterbible.org, means, "having nothing to strike against, not causing to stumble, and, not leading others to sin by one's mode of life." Blameless implies that believers are not to succumb to sinful conduct. Their goal is to spur others on toward love and good deeds (Hebrews 10:24). Blameless followers live with a clear conscience (2 Timothy 1:3). Their hearts go out to those who do not know the Lord so they are never interested in pleasing themselves. They would rather seek out the good of others (1 Corinthians 10:33) to hopefully lead them to Christ. Blameless believers never lead people astray with their words or actions. They would never want to cause anyone to stumble or fall. Along with Paul, believers would say, "Our conscience testifies that we have conducted ourselves in the world, and especially in our relations with you, with integrity and godly sincerity. We have done so, relying not on worldly wisdom but on God's grace" (2 Corinthians 1:12).

When pure and blameless are combined in this context, the Lord is commanding all believers to live with inward integrity before the Lord and have external integrity before man. Is this at all possible for Christians to accomplish in their own strength? No. Fortunately,

God has sent His Spirit to indwell and fill followers of Christ because we are hopeless without Him. Therefore, through the power of the Holy Spirit, Christians are more than capable of living a pure and blameless life.

It is becoming more and more evident that our world needs Christians being more influential in their workplaces, schools, and communities. Without a doubt, the church should be the one place that teaches about living a pure and blameless life. Pastors should hold their members accountable to these standards so they can grow spiritually mature. That's why Paul says, "So Christ himself gave the apostles, the prophets, the evangelists, the pastors and teachers, to equip his people for works of service, so that the body of Christ may be built up until we all reach unity in the faith and in the knowledge of the Son of God and become mature, attaining to the whole measure of the fullness of Christ" (Ephesians 4:11-13). The Bible is clear that the church is only part of the maturing process.

Moses, on the other hand, says, "Impress them on your children. Talk about them when you sit at home and when you walk along the road, when you lie down and when you get up" (Deuteronomy 6:7). True followers of Christ need to learn God's Word through their own personal study, devote themselves to a church where the Bible is properly taught, then live out their pure and blameless lifestyle in the workplace, school, and especially in the home. There is no greater place to model how to live a pure and blameless life than with the people you're with the most: your family. This is a critical truth for parents.

Do moms and dads understand the command to "impress" God's commands on the lives of their children? Some do. But based on the current cultural landscape there is cause to believe many do not. We are in a cultural crisis when it comes to people living a pure and blameless life. There are countless reasons for this deficiency in our world today. But one of the main causes for our cultural demise is the lack of integrity in the home. Parents are living unrighteous lives and are oblivious to the short term and long term effects it has on their children. What causes this? I believe parents grossly underestimate the influence they have in the lives of their kids.

Way, way back in 1967...I know you don't remember...television stations were required by law to run one anti-smoking commercial for every three cigarette commercials. One of the antismoking commercials begins with a father painting his home on top of a ladder that's leaning against his house. The camera slowly pans downward to show his young son painting away just like his dad on a much smaller ladder also leaning against the house. As the father and son team work on their project together, a voiceover announcer makes the statement, "Like father, like son." The next scene shows the father and son duo driving down the street in their Ford Mustang convertible: the dad behind the wheel and his son safely beside him in the customized car seat, complete with his own steering wheel. As they approach an intersection, the father puts his arm out of the window to signal to other drivers that he is about to make a left turn. Without hesitation, the son quickly copies his dad's hand signal and makes the same gesture outside his window. Next we see the father-son pair giving their Mustang a bath. In the background, the dad has a rag in one hand and a hosepipe in the other. The father is washing and rinsing the driver's side front fender. In the foreground the son is stooped low beside the passenger's side front tire. Just like dad, the son is working hard on the tire with his sponge for cleaning and a squirt gun for rinsing. As the two enjoy working together, the boy playfully pops up from his squatted position and surprises the dad by shooting him with his squirt gun. As the commercial continues, the father and son twosome are together taking a leisurely walk in their neighborhood. The dad sees a rock, bends down, picks up the rock, and tosses it into some woods. Just like his father, the son also finds a rock and throws it into the same patch of woods. The commercial's final scene has the tired father and son pair sitting next to a tree resting from their busy day of activities. The father reaches into his shirt pocket and pulls out a pack of cigarettes. He takes out a cigarette, lays down the pack beside his son, puts the cigarette to his lips, strikes a match, and lights it while his son quietly sits beside him observing his every move. As expected, the son looks down at the pack of cigarettes, picks it up, and curiously looks into the pack as if to mimic what he has just seen his father do. As the boy examines the cigarette pack, this time the voiceover announcer asks a question, "like father, like son? Think about it!"

Like it or not, believe it or not, this 1960's commercial is unbelievably accurate regarding the copycat nature of children. It is amazing how much influence parents have on their kids. This advertisement depicts the truth that children can and will imitate the things they see and hear, especially when displayed by their parents. Now my question is simply this: what do your kids see and hear from you that they imitate? It is probably more than you think.

More times than not, children do what they see their parents do. "The apple doesn't fall far from the tree," and "a chip off the old block" are very true sayings. These illustrate the incredible comparisons between parents and their children. There are numerous similarities in looks, demeanors, and inclinations that can be uncanny. From a spiritual standpoint, however, it is astonishing to see the parallels in the parents' spiritual maturity levels and that of their children. In his book, *Parenting with Kingdom Purpose*, Ken Hemphill drove home this point when he said, "Most parents who want to know where their kids are headed religiously just need to look in the mirror." In many cases, the spiritual levels of the parents and their kids are remarkably related.

God has deliberately placed each child in the lives of their parents. There is no mistake. His goal is for moms and dads to prepare them to live out each day with integrity to honor Him. Discipleship with every child begins at home. God's design is to have every child living with the most influential people in their lives to constantly talk with them concerning God, help them properly think about God, and show them how to carefully obey God. In the end, parents are ultimately responsible for preparing them for eternity. Let that sink in! Therefore, if children, especially teenagers, are ever going to experience a healthy relationship with the Lord, they need moms and dads to be living inwardly pure and outwardly blameless lives of integrity.

Needless to say, this is a serious matter. Parents can ill afford to take living a life of integrity for granted. They must faithfully be continual learners of the Word of God and deliberately live it out with consistency. Why? Scott McConnell observed, "Students are experts at noticing inconsistencies between what parents say and do." It is easy for parents to talk the talk, but the real issue comes down to can they walk the walk. Norma Schmidt stated, "My mother had put her finger on an essential truth: Kids absorb the values they see adults putting into action. Ever notice how quickly kids spot any inconsistency between what we say and what we do? Long before kids can spell 'hypocrisy,' they notice when our actions fall short of our words." "Don't worry that children never listen to you; worry that they are always watching you," author Robert Fulghum says. Kids need to see us 'walking the talk.' In fact, we teach kids best when we practice being what we want to see in them." Parents need to understand that hypocrisy is a serious issue. Nothing undermines a mom's and dad's efforts in training their children in righteousness than when their actions and God's commands do not match up.

John Maxwell put it another way when he said, "we teach what we know, we reproduce what we are." By and large, what parents think about subjects, what they say concerning issues, and how they respond to circumstances often are adopted by their children. Christian Smith in his book *Soul Searching*, stated, "We'll get what we are. By normal processes of socialization, and unless other significant forces intervene, more than what parents might say they want as religious outcomes in their children, most parents most likely will end up getting religiously of their children what they themselves are." Living a pure and blameless life may require parents to make major adjustments in their thoughts, words, and actions. Parents, need to focus first on their own personal pursuit of God. The bottom line is this: moms and dads reproduce themselves in their kids whether they like it or not.[2]

Moses and Paul have made it an absolute command for all believers, especially parents, to live with integrity. Living a pure and blameless life is essential. James also contributes by challenging Christians when he says, "Do not merely listen to the word, and so deceive yourselves. Do (imperative mood) what it says" (James 1:22). These men make it abundantly clear that people who call themselves followers of Christ are to live differently than those who have not put their trust and faith in Jesus. John states, "Whoever claims to live in him must live as Jesus did" (1 John 2:6). What is the Lord desiring? Simple. He wants His people to learn His Word and then do it with integrity. When Moses said, "be on your guard (imperative mood) and

---

[2] Mark Smith, *Parental Guidance Suggested* (L'Edge Press, 2012), 16, 41.

diligently watch (imperative mood) yourselves" (Deuteronomy 4:9) he, along with the rest, was giving an absolute command to be an authentic doer of scripture. Hope comes alive when Christians surrender to these standards.

Question for the Pastor, Leader, Teacher reading this book: Integrity is a critical issue in our culture today. Our homes need moms and dads living an authentic life now more than ever. Are you teaching how to live a pure and blameless life to your congregation... Are you living it yourself first?

CHAPTER 4
TEACH (Part 1)

"Impress them on your children…" Deuteronomy 6:7a

Not too many years ago I was standing outside the church's student center welcoming teenagers and their friends to our Wednesday night youth event. I always tried to greet each teen as he or she came into the building. One night two dads walked into the student center each with his teenager in tow. Without hesitation, I greeted the fathers and their children. We engaged in some small talk, and they went inside the building. It was refreshing to see these men leading their kids to church on a Wednesday night. I remember the thought running through my mind that these men were being great examples to their teens. Ten minutes later, as I was still welcoming arriving students, the same two dads walked past me on their way to the parking lot. This time they didn't stop to chat. As they walked past me, I overheard one of them say, "We've got an hour; want to go get something to drink?" My earlier warm thoughts and feelings drained right out of me! I was speechless! As I watched them get into a car and pull out of the parking lot, several questions ran through my mind. Why were these fathers dropping off their teens and then leaving? Why were they not staying? We had adult programs running at the same time we had our youth event. Why didn't they go to one of those? Needless to say, I felt reduced from being a youth pastor to a babysitter.

After that night I knew there was something wrong, but I wasn't exactly sure what it was. Over the course of several days and weeks I went to scripture in search of the answer. After pouring through numerous passages, the Lord showed me a single verse. Nestled just after the Shama, the Lord describes and defines His perfect plan for parents and their families. The Lord says through Moses, "Impress them on your children." This may appear to be a simple phrase with little meaning but don't let it fool you. It speaks incredible volumes.

The New International Version Bible translates the first word of Deuteronomy chapter six verse seven as "impress." Other Bible translations render the beginning of the verse as "repeat them" (HCSB), "repeat them again and again" (NLT), and "teach them diligently" (KJV, NKJV, NASB, ESV). In the original Hebrew language, the root word is actually shanan which means "to teach and to sharpen". However, what makes shanan such a unique and poignant word in this text is how the Lord led Moses to use it grammatically. Just before Israel was to leave the desert and enter into the Promise Land, their determined leader pronounced shanan with the "piel" stem.

Now before you start yawning and your eyes glaze over with sheer boredom from this Hebrew lesson, hang in there with me for just a few minutes. There is a method to this madness. The reason I bring up all these seemingly insignificant details is because there is great beauty and power in what seems to be meaningless.

Moses is not the only one the Holy Spirit led to use the word shanan in scripture. Solomon, Isaiah, David, and other psalmists use the verb shanan in their writings. But Moses, in Deuteronomy 6:7, is the only one in the entire Bible who uses this word in the piel form. When any verb has a piel stem the word has an intensive or intentional action. For instance, the phrase "he broke the glass" when spoken in the piel voice literally means "he smashed the glass to pieces." When the root word shanan, which means to teach and to sharpen, is combined with the intensity of the piel verb form this important word takes on a special meaning for parents. What we find is God commanding parents to intensively teach their children His perfect and infallible Word. God instructs moms and dads to intentionally sharpen their kids with scripture for all of life's challenges. Moses pulls no punches with this word. He emphasizes the importance of parents being proactive as they prepare their children to encounter each day equipped with the principles of God's Word.

But that's not all. Moses expounds on the word shanan in the remaining portion of verse seven to take the verb to a deeper level. With the idea of parents intensively teaching and intentionally sharpening their children with the Word of God, the frequency of their teaching and sharpening is also crucial.

Just after Moses commands us to "impress" God's Word into the lives of our children, he gives instruction on how to actually make that happen within the rhythm of each day. He says, "Talk about them when you sit at home and when you walk along the road, when you lie down and when you get up" (Deuteronomy 6:7b). What's God's prophet talking about? Simply, as the primary disciplers, the Lord has given moms and dads the privilege and responsibility to intentionally engage their children daily in something known as faith talks.

Faith talks are those times throughout the day parents can intentionally discuss an aspect of scripture the Lord is using in their lives or in the life of their child. One example is having a conversation about the pastor's Sunday morning sermon. Helping children apply the points of the message to their lives at school will allow them to connect the Bible to everyday life. Faith talks are times when moms and dads are driving down the road and something comes on the radio that could be used to spark a spiritual conversation. Parents could talk about the lyrics of the last song that was played on the radio and discuss how the message of the song promotes or discredits Christlike living. Another way to intentionally discuss scripture is while parents are putting their children to bed. With simple questions moms and dads can help their kids process the activities of the day from a Biblical perspective. For instance, parents could ask, "What spiritual significance did you see in the movie we just watched?" Faith talks are devotions parents have with their kids at breakfast before everyone heads off for the day. There are countless ways to have faith talks. Object lessons, upcoming holidays, special events, etc.. can provide great opportunities to talk about the Lord. But the key to faith talks is they need to take place daily.

The objective of faith talks is for moms and dads to frequently, strategically, and purposefully have discussions about God's Word with those precious gifts the Lord has entrusted to them. However, there is one important aspect of the faith talk strategy I need to mention. Proactive parents need to regularly use faith talks on simple topics to help them segue into more in-depth topics and harder teachings of God's Word. In other words, parents need to connect with their kids on basic issues so they can connect with them on deeper levels. Why? Children need to be constantly prepared for the intense battles they face each and every day. Keep in mind, the overarching goal of faith talks is to help kids be more firmly rooted in their faith. The writer of Hebrews puts it best when he says, "Anyone who lives on milk, being still an infant, is not acquainted with the teaching about righteousness. But solid food is for the mature, who by constant use have trained themselves to distinguish good from evil" (Hebrews 5:13-14). Faith talks need to be well thought out, practical, Biblically based, relevant concepts related to today's tough life issues. They need to be interwoven with basic as well as deep Biblical concepts to better develop each child spiritually. But most importantly they need to be done consistently.

Teaching and sharpening children takes time but most importantly it requires repetition. At this point you may be thinking, "How can busy parents be obedient to the Lord and, at the same time, pass along their faith to their children?" The answer comes back to one simple, key word: intentionality.

I have found that moms and dads always have enough time for the things they have to do. They will even make time to do the things they like to do. But I have found everyone has to be intentional to do the things that are hard to do. Teaching kids spiritual truths can feel like a daunting task. There are always obstacles. The road is never easy, but as long as God is on the throne there is always hope. When dedicated and determined parents intentionally give of themselves to instruct and hone their children with God's Word, nothing will compare to the benefits. The rewards moms and dads will receive are eternal. Never stop sharpening…their life depends on it.

Let's look at it this way. A soldier prepared himself for combat in many ways. One of the ways he made himself ready was to inspect his equipment to insure each piece was in perfect condition to give him the greatest chance of victory. Before going into battle, the soldier would take a sharpening stone to hone the blade of his sword. He would carefully place the surface of the stone on one side of the blade and repeatedly stroke that side of his blade. Then he would repeat the process on the opposite side. Intensively and intentionally the soldier would work on his weapon, alternating from one side to the other, until his blade was razor sharp and ready for battle. After the soldier returned from battle, he would inspect and clean his equipment again. To prepare for the next altercation, he would take his sword and meticulously repeat the honing process to have his saber ready for the next encounter. Sharpening takes a great deal of time, but every second proves to be well worth the repetitious effort.

Like sharpening a sword, when parents regularly have Biblically based faith talks, their children will be sharper and better able to stand against the onslaught of the world's battles. Sharpening children may take a lot of time and a great deal of intentionality on the part of parents, but the rewards are endless.

Not only are faith talks an important component in making long-lasting disciples of children; taking advantage of God moments are vital too. Like faith talks, God moments are for the sole purpose of leading children into a deeper love relationship with the Father. However, the difference of a faith talk from a God moment lies in the fact that it cannot be planned. The frequency of a God moment does not depend on the parent. The God moment occurs when the Lord decides.

Usually out of nowhere, He shows up and then shows off. He just happens to be where you are in an unexpected way at an unexpected time. He shows up in a phone call from the doctor. He shows up in a breaking news report. He shows up in the grandeur of a mountain landscape. He shows up in a random act of kindness. It's in those moments the Lord is giving moms and dads a unique opportunity to see Him from a different perspective and give them the opportunity to talk about Him in a new way.

Without a doubt, these are special glimpses with which the Lord blesses us. However, they come with a warning. They can be easily missed. When our schedules are overloaded and we're too busy, when we're pre-occupied with our own needs, or when we are unfocused spiritually, God can be right in front of us and we will not even see Him. We can be blinded. That's why it is so important for pastors, leaders, teachers, and especially parents to have margin in their lives. Parents' eyes and hearts need to be trained to see and anticipate the daily movement of God in and around their lives. When they expectantly keep themselves attuned to the interactiveness of the Lord in their own lives through prayer and Bible study, He will show Himself in some unbelievable, unforgettable, and teachable moments. These are the moments that bring hope to our families.

There is nothing easy about becoming or maintaining the proactive parent mindset. Being a shanan type of disciple maker really comes down to determination. Daily faith talks and waiting on God moments to occur are simple yet effective tools the Lord can use to give parents the opportunity to intensively teach and intentionally sharpen their children. Moses' special use of shanan is a specific instruction to parents to make discipleship a natural part of their home. When you look into the Hebrew language and do an in depth study of the nuances of the word shanan we see the Bible's command to parents more clearly. Is God calling parents to a higher standard?

Question for the Pastor, Leader, Teacher reading this book: Are you willing to model and teach the parents of your congregation how to make discipleship within their home a priority? This may require you to model and teach them how to have margin in their lives so they can have faith talks and be ready for God moments. The next generations need your example today!

CHAPTER 5
TEACH (Part 2)

"Teach them to your children..." Deuteronomy 11:19a

Zach Bumgarner was a former student in my youth ministry. During high school he was a three sport letterman playing football, basketball, and baseball. By his sophomore year, Zach was making his presence known as a starter on the varsity football team. After graduation, Zach received a scholarship to play football at the University of North Carolina, Charlotte. At six foot four, two hundred and sixty-eight pounds he was quickly positioned on the offensive line. Zack is a beast.

Periodically I try to catch up with Zach to see how the team is doing, what his classes are like, and what the Lord is doing in his life. Without fail, our conversations about the team and school go quickly. We spend the majority of our time talking about what God is doing in and through his life. What a praise!

One day I was doing some scripture reading on the "Teach" aspect of the Learn – Do – Teach methodology. My study was focused on how parents can help their children learn God's Word. As I meditated on different passages, the Lord gave me an idea on how to best communicate and illustrate this important concept. I quickly realized this analogy would help moms and dads better understand the essence of being a proactive parent.

Before I took my next breath, I was thumbing through the contact list on my phone to find Zach's number. I had a burning question that needed to be answered. He was barely able to get the words "Hey Mark" out of his mouth before I interrupted him and asked, "How does your coach teach your football team new plays?" I know for Zach this was an abrupt beginning to the normal protocol of our conversations, but this was urgent.

Zach was gracious and without hesitation began to answer. He described how his coach will take a notepad, scratch paper, or a napkin to design a new offensive play. He draws a rough sketch of the play with the traditional X's and O's, full of lines, and arrows. The X's and O's show where each player is to be positioned on the field and the lines and arrows describe blocking assignments or what direction a player is to run. Every mark on the page has a purpose.

The coach gathers the offensive team together in a classroom and takes them through four important steps to get them ready for game day. His first step is to distribute the well-crafted play (a final draft) to each member of the offense. The coach discusses how the play works, what situation it needs to be run in, what defense it would work best against, etc... His goal is to thoroughly explain the play until his players have a solid grasp of how it works. The coach is insistent that the players be as knowledgeable of the play as he is. After class, they are expected to study and memorize the coach's design just as they have memorized all the other previously introduced plays.

After each player understands their responsibility and how to execute the play properly, they go out to the practice field for the second step. The offensive unit lines up in their positions and does what is called a "walk-through." Each player stands in his designated spot and simply walks to the proper location prescribed by the play. The players are so proficient, you would think the coach had drawn the lines and arrows on the grass. This is the second most critical point in the process. The team is now taking the playbook and putting it into motion but in the safe confines of their private practice facility. When all the players have been sufficiently drilled and the coach is satisfied with their performance, he has the offense put on their practice uniform for the third step. This is the most critical part of the practice.

Fully dressed with pads and helmets, the coach has his offensive players set up to run their new play. This time, however, they are faced by the defensive unit. They run the play half speed, three quarter speed, then full speed until they have worked out all the kinks and can execute the play to perfection. The coach has his team run and re-run the same play because repetition is the key.

The coach isn't satisfied until his team has studied the playbook, done a walk through, and flawlessly run the play in a mock situation. After the offense has mastered the play, the team is now ready to implement their new weapon when the opportunity presents itself in an up-coming game.

Zach went on to mention a fourth part of their process – the accountability. He told me that there are points during the game when the offense is off the field or at half-time the coach can make any necessary adjust-ments (or chastise a player). After their contest, the team gets the chance to watch game film the following week to critique all their plays and learn where they need to improve.

I could not believe what I was hearing. It was fascinat-ing to hear Zach describe how his coach prepared the team to run new plays for a football game. But what re-ally blew me away was how this approach can be imple-mented by parents in their homes. The principles are the same. Zach laid out an excellent model for moms and dads to follow in their efforts to intentionally dis-ciple their children.

The coach used the two methods of teaching Moses describes in the book of Deuteronomy. It's easy to see the first method he used. As you recall from chapter four, the Hebrew word shanan means to intensively and intentionally teach in a repetitive way. The coach employed the shanan teaching style to introduce his offense to their new play. In the classroom the coach would draw and redraw the play on the marker-board to teach his players his new offensive strategy. In their personal study time, the players would commit the play to memory for later use in practice and on game day. On the practice field, they would run and rerun the play until it was perfectly executed. Repetition was one of the key ingredients he used to teach his team. Understandably, this technique made the new play become second-nature to the team.

However, did you also notice the second method the coach used to help his players learn the new play? He knew his players gather information in one of three basic ways - visually, auditorially, or kinestheticly. He used these three methods to teach his team. Educators refer to these three primary ways of learning as learning styles. Moses, on the other hand, calls this the lamad teaching style.

The Bible says, "Teach them to your children, talking about them when you sit at home and when you walk along the road, when you lie down and when you get up" (Deuteronomy 11:19). Much like shanan, the word "Teach" in this verse has a special meaning. Moses used the Hebrew word lamad with the piel stem to intensify and give it an intentional action. As you remember from chapter four, the phrase "he broke the glass" when spoken in the piel voice literally means "he smashed the glass to pieces." When you combine the root word lamad, to teach, with the intensity of the piel verb form the definition of "teach" becomes "to cause to learn."

The phrase "to cause to learn" leaves us with a question. How do you cause someone to learn? There is only one way to discover the answer to this puzzling question – the Bible. King Solomon gave us some fatherly advice to consider in scripture. The Bible says, "Train up a child in the way he should go: and when he is old, he will not depart from it" (Prov. 22:6 KJV).

"Train" in the original Hebrew language is chanak. According to David Jeremiah this word has a unique meaning. He said, "An Arab midwife would rub crushed dates on the palate of a baby's mouth to stimulate the instinctive action to suck, so that the child could be nourished. Over time the concept of training up came to mean 'to create a thirst or a hunger within a child for the godly things of life.'"[3]

The phrase translated "in the way" is the Hebrew word derek. Chuck Swindoll, in his book *Parenting: From Surviving to Thriving*, gave excellent insight into the word derek. He said, "One visual image associated with derek is that of an archer's bow, which has a natural curvature to it… Each child, like a bow, comes with a shape, or a bent, that is natural to him or her. If a bow is to be useful, it cannot remain in its natural, relaxed state. An archer must work with the bow's characteristic curvature, so he can bend the wood in the right direction, and string it so that it might become a source of power."[4]

---

[3] Mark Smith, *Parental Guidance Suggested* (L'Edge Press, 2012), 99.
[4] Ibid.

Each person has a unique coding that enables him or her to learn. It was evident that Zach's coach understood this principle well. Did you catch how the coach handed out a diagram of the play drawn on a piece of paper? Did you also notice how the coach used the marker board in the classroom? These tactics were strategically aimed at his visual learners. When a visual learner can see the X's, O's, and arrows illustrated on paper or white board their comprehension level increases. Did you note how the coach also had a meeting with the team to talk about how the play works, what situation it needs to be run in, what defense it would work best against, etc…? Most likely there was a two-way exchange allowing the players to discuss and ask the coach questions. For an auditory learner this brings learning to life. Not only was there a visual aspect to the teaching time the coach also utilized verbal communication. After the notebooks were closed and the classroom time was complete, it was time to put the play into motion. Perhaps this was the most important component of the teaching process for the kinesthetic learners. The coach physically engaged the team in walk-throughs. After the walk throughs, he slowly worked them up to running the play full speed. This is a beautiful picture of the lamad style of teaching in action and what it looks like to cause someone to learn. (See Appendix – 1 for more information on learning styles.)

Like the coach, parents should consider using Moses' two teaching approaches. The coach was intentional, intensive, and repetitive. He also studied his player's natural makeup, tendencies, and habits of learning. By tapping into both the shanan and lamad styles of teaching the coach was able to customize a strategy to get his team better prepared for game day. The beauty of these teaching styles is they both can be implemented into the natural flow of a family's life. In other words...hope for the family.

Questions for the Pastor, Leader, Teacher reading this book: With all the new ideas, Hebrew words, and illustrations flying around, I have to stop and ask a few questions. How well do you think parents are preparing their children for game day? Most likely some more than others. But is that good enough? Doesn't it seem like everyday gets more challenging for Christians? Does today appear more filled with temptation than yesterday? Are children today living in a world that is darker than the one their parents grew up in? Perhaps the wrong questions are being asked. Instead of asking how well are moms and dads preparing their kids for game day, maybe we need to ask this question: How well is the church equipping the parents (Ephesians 4:11-12) to be the primary disciple-makers of their homes?

Now the tough question is, "Are you willing to educate your parents on how to teach their children by using the shanan and lamad teaching styles?" Not only does the next generation need you but every generation needs you.

Note: See Appendix – 2 for more information on how to cultivate a solid faith foundation in the home.

CHAPTER 6
THE FUTURE

"...hear my words so that they may learn to revere me as long as they live in the land and may teach them to their children." (Deuteronomy 4:10b)

My wife and I are empty nesters and loving it. Now before you get the wrong idea and begin judging us, let me assure you of one important fact. We adore our two children, Abby and Adam, but the Lord didn't give them to us to keep them in our house forever. God gave us the responsibility to introduce them to His Son. He allowed us the awesome privilege of raising them in the way they should go. Most importantly, the Lord commissioned us to launch them into the world to be disciple-makers. God has given them wonderful spouses, and they are serving the Lord in great churches. We love our relationship with our adult children and always enjoy the time we get to spend with them. Even though our home life is significantly different, we would not change it for anything.

Since it is just the two of us, we have settled into a much different routine than when our children were at home.

Instead of completing homework, going to sporting events, or attending school activities, our evenings have a much different pace. We enjoy cooking meals, playing board games, sitting on our deck, and watching television together. Life is simple. Life is great!

One evening after dinner, Sherri and I cleaned up the dishes and got ourselves ready for one of our favorite TV shows. The episode that night was entitled, "The Alchemist." The show that night was engaging and entertaining as expected; however, the episode's title got my attention. I had heard the word "Alchemist" before, but I wasn't exactly sure of it's meaning. This sent me into an all-out fact-finding mission to discover the details of this word.

According to dictionary.com, alchemist is a noun which means "a person who is versed in or practices alchemy." Since that wasn't helpful, I continued digging and found that the word alchemy has an interesting definition. Dictionary.com says,

> "al-kuh-mee— noun, plural al·che·mies
>
> 1 – a form of chemistry and speculative philosophy practiced in the Middle Ages and the Renaissance and concerned principally with discovering methods for transmuting baser metals into gold and with finding a universal solvent and an elixir of life.

2 – any magical power or process of transmuting a common substance, usually of little value, into a substance of great value."

This word really began to spark my interest, especially the part about "transmuting a common substance into a substance of great value." As I continued my investigation, I broadened the scope of my search to other regions of the Internet. Needless to say I had a lot to sift through. To say the World Wide Web had an abundance of information is an understatement. There was plenty. But to get a clear understanding of who the alchemists were and what they did I needed to start with the word's origin.

Etymologists have discovered that alchemy was a common part of the Old French, Medieval Latin, and Arabic languages. Many scholars believe alchemy was derived from the Greek word "khymeia" which means "that which is poured out." They also speculate that the word may have first been used in the pharmaceutical chemistry profession. It appears that early on an alchemist's job entailed mixing juices or infusing plants in liquids for medicinal purposes.

After having a better understanding of its roots, I found other bits of trivia about the people who practiced alchemy quite interesting. Throughout the centuries, alchemists were known for their deep commitment to their art and for having an unquenchable desire to make a difference in the world. While many outsiders saw them as magicians or a secret society, they were hard workers who had high aspirations. However, there was one thing that plagued these unique scientists. Their accomplishments were almost nonexistent. For example, every attempt of turning metals like lead into gold ended in utter disappointment. They also tried for years to mix the right ingredients to concoct a "wonder potion" that would cure all that ailed you. But that too ended in an epic failure.

On a positive note, we can say their efforts were not totally in vain. Alchemists were given credit for their discovery of the chemical element phosphorus. This relentless bunch was also given praise for the refinement of many lab techniques that are still in use today. Their contributions were not a part of their original plans, but at least the alchemists of yesteryear were able to give science something worthwhile to remember them by.

Instead of focusing on who the alchemists were or what they did or did not accomplish, I would rather focus on what fueled their fire. Alchemists were a driven crowd with tremendous ambition. When you put who they were and what they attempted to accomplish into simple terms, these people desired to make something better than it was before. We can boil down their intentions into one simple term – improvement.

My intent is not to replace or strip away the original definition. Instead, my goal is to highlight the positive aspects of alchemy and give it a new purpose from a Christian perspective. When we redefine alchemy as, "making something better or improving something" and approach it from a Biblical worldview, we can produce a new phrase with a richer meaning - Christian alchemist. You may be wondering, "What is a Christian alchemist?"

The basic definition of a Christian alchemist is a person who:

> ...*authentically loves* the Lord with all their heart, soul, and strength. (Deuteronomy 6:5)

> ...*invests in others* to make them better than they were before. (Matthew 5:14,16)

> ...is not only a listener of God's Word but a *doer of God's Word.* (James 1:22)

> ...*constantly strives to live a life of integrity.* (Philippians 1:9-10)

It's important that we put some meat on the bones of the basic definition. To help us understand what a Christian alchemist is and what they do, we need to expand the four descriptions and apply a few corresponding verses. This will allow our new phrase to take shape and come alive.

Authentically Loves

Moses commanded the Israelites, "Love the LORD your God with all your heart and with all your soul and with all your strength" (Deuteronomy 6:5).

Christian alchemists authentically love the Lord with every aspect of their lives. They are forgiven. Their lives have been redeemed. These people has been born again, indwelled by the Holy Spirt, and strive to stay filled with the Spirit. They are keenly aware they have been bought with a price. Some would say Christian alchemist are committed to the Lord. However, the word committed doesn't do the Christian alchemist justice. They have surrendered their heart, surrendered their soul, and surrendered their strength to the Lord. Their authentic love drives them to be slaves (doulos) of God.

Invests in Others

> Jesus said to the crowd, "You are the light of the world. A town built on a hill cannot be hidden….In the same way, let your light shine before others, that they may see your good deeds and glorify your Father in heaven" (Matthew 5:14, 16).

Christian alchemists have a burning desire to let their lights shine in this very dark world. Their lives are guided and empowered by the Holy Spirt to dispel the darkness with the brilliant light of the Gospel. Their mission is simple. Christian alchemists want to pour their lives into others. They patiently and expectantly wait for the opportunity to share with others how they too can have a personal relationship with Jesus. Then they faithfully invest their time and energy in people by helping them grow as disciples of Christ. They are tenaciously driven individuals who want to help others live their lives better than they did before.

A Doer of God's Word

"Do not merely listen to the word, and so deceive yourselves. Do what it says" (James 1:22).

Nothing holds back Christian alchemists from being doers of God's Word. There is no compromise. They study the Bible; they have a passionate desire to be obedient to scripture; and they implement God's commands into every aspect of their lives. They are not perfect people, but that is their goal. Christian alchemists will strive to be a disciplined follower of Christ for the sole purpose of bringing glory to the Father.

Strives to Live a Life of Integrity

Paul said, "And this is my prayer: that your love may abound more and more in knowledge and depth of insight, so that you may be able to discern what is best and may be pure and blameless for the day of Christ" (Philippians 1:9-10).

Christian alchemists take integrity very seriously. They hold nothing back when it comes to a pure and blameless life. Christian alchemists are sensitive to the sin in their lives. They will always allow the light of God's Word to expose any sin in their lives. Covering up sin is not an option. Hypocrisy is also a word that is foreign to them. They are constantly on guard to maintain a close walk with the Lord. Above all, Christian alchemists are disciplined to study God's Word, pray without ceasing, and never tire of doing good works. They have an unquenchable thirst to live with inward integrity before the Lord and have external integrity before man. It is contagious.

My guess is as a pastor, leader, and teacher you possess all of the qualities of a Christian alchemist but didn't know what to call yourself. I am sure you would agree that every follower of Jesus Christ should be this intentional. Parents, grandparents, and children who have put their trust and faith in Christ can be change agents in their homes now and for future generations. Being a Christian alchemist isn't about changing the next generation. It's about changing every generation.

It comes down to one important question. Will you say, "yes?" As a pastor, leader, teacher, will you allow the Lord to pour Himself into your life so you can spill out into the lives of others? You can say "no." You don't have to buy into this new phrase and it's meaning or the entire Proactive Parenting philosophy. But I have to ask, why would you say no to being a Christian alchemist? Consider these questions:

- Are you okay with the current direction our culture is heading?
- Is your church doing enough to educate parents about how the media manipulates their children?
- Does your church discuss the adverse effects of materialism on our society?
- Are you willing to sit and watch another generation be raised up not knowing the Lord?

If you had a negative response to any of these questions, you may want to consider a change - a change in emphasis…a change in strategy…a change to become a Christian alchemist.

Consider this story told by Soren Kierkegaard. There is a little town of ducks. Every Sunday the ducks waddle out of their houses and waddle down Main Street to their church. They waddle into the sanctuary and squat in their proper pews. The duck choir waddles in and takes its place. Then the duck minister comes forward and opens the duck Bible (Ducks, like all other creatures on earth, seem to have their own special version of the Scriptures.) He reads to them: "Ducks! God has given you wings! With wings you can fly! With wings you can mount up and soar like eagles. No walls can confine you! No fences can hold you! You have wings. God has given you wings and you can fly like birds!" All the ducks shout "Amen!" And then they all waddle home.

Waddling requires nothing - no action - no change. However, soaring requires transformation - complete abandonment - total surrender. Being a Christian alchemist means you're refusing to waddle - no more sticking your head in the sand. You will not give up! What you're actually saying is that you will strive to:

- Encourage parents to be serious students of God's Word (Learn)
- Lead and challenge parents to live a pure and blameless lives of integrity (Do)
- Encourage the shanan and lamad teaching styles in the homes of your congregation (Teach)
- Inspire parents to wisely lead their homes with the future in mind

Now that's hope!

Question for the Pastor, Leader, Teacher reading this book: Simple question… Are you willing to de-program your church and implement the Learn - Do - Teach Proactive Parenting philosophy in your congregation?

APPENDIX 1
LEARNING STYLES

How do your kids learn best?

It is important to remember the fatherly advice Solomon gave parents regarding their task as the primary disciplers. The Bible says, "Train up a child in the way he should go: and when he is old, he will not depart from it" (Prov. 22:6 KJV). Looking back to Day 3 we discussed the word "train." "Train" in the original Hebrew language is chanak. According to David Jeremiah this word has a unique meaning. He said, "An Arab midwife would rub crushed dates on the palate of a baby's mouth to stimulate the instinctive action to suck, so that the child could be nourished. Over time the concept of training up came to mean 'to create a thirst or a hunger within a child for the godly things of life.'" God gives parents the awesome privilege of cultivating a hunger and a thirst in their child's lives regarding spiritual things. How can parents, who are believers in Jesus Christ, help create a spiritual appetite for the Lord in their kids? I don't know many parents who do not desire for their children to have a growing relationship with the Lord. But most parents have no idea where to start, or they give up soon after making a few failed attempts and lose all confidence. It's like trying to hit a target when you don't know where to aim.

Do you remember the Peanuts cartoon? Charles Schultz, creator of Charlie Brown and the gang, was one of the world's best social critics and theologians to every live. For years, the Peanuts cartoon was his platform to make commentary concerning culture and teach biblical truth. One of Schultz's classic cartoons had Charlie Brown at summer camp. He and the other campers were at the archery range. A camper comments on Charlie Brown's incredible ability to hit so many of the bulls-eyes. Charlie Brown says, "Well, I do it a little differently. I first shoot the arrow and then I go and draw a bulls-eye around where it hits." That's one way to build confidence. Drawing bulls-eyes after you shoot your arrow always guarantees hitting the mark. I know a few parents who wish discipleship was that easy. At any rate, the question has to be asked again: how can parents generate a hunger for discipleship in each of their children? How can parents properly aim at the right target and hit it with confidence? The answer, of course, is found in the Bible.

The Bible has all the answers and interestingly enough, the answer is found in the same verse we've been discussing. The phrase translated "in the way" is the Hebrew word derek. According to blueletterbible.com the phrase means, "way, road, distance, journey, manner, path, journey, direction, manner, habit, of course of life (fig.), of moral character (fig.)." Chuck Swindoll in his book, Parenting: From Surviving to Thriving, gave excellent insight into the word derek. He said, One visual image associated with derek is that of an archer's bow, which has a natural curvature to it… Each child, like a bow, comes with a shape, or a bent, that is natural to him or her. If a bow is to be useful, it cannot remain in its natural, relaxed state. An archer must work with the bow's characteristic curvature, so he can bend the wood in the right direction, and string it so that it might become a source of power.

Not only are parents responsible for producing a hunger and a thirst in their kids, the Bible commands that they create this desire through their natural "bent." John White, of Bible.org, made this statement concerning Proverbs 22:6. He stated, Solomon urges parents to learn well the unique traits of their children. He knew that spiritual training, to be effective, must be "coded" differently for each child so the child will embrace it and, as he or she matures, be shaped by it.

Does such an understanding render this great verse toothless? Hardly. What it does is give parents the challenge of their lives—to shape God's truth into a well-aimed arrow that hits the mark deep in the heart of a child!

His commentary sheds a new perspective on the word derek. Each child has a unique coding that enables him or her to learn. Parents should consider studying their kid's natural makeup, tendencies, and habits of learning and then customize their discipleship strategy. As primary disciplers, it is so important to discover your child's natural bent as a learner in order to know how to best disciple them.

God has designed every person uniquely, and He loves for people to gain knowledge about Him, the world, and themselves. However, people receive and process information differently. Children and teens gather information in one of three basic ways called learning styles. Educators describe the three learning styles as visual, auditory, and kinesthetic. These different learning styles are explained in detail below:

Visual learners process new information by reading, looking at graphics, or watching a demonstration. Children with this learning style can grasp information presented in a chart or graph, but they may grow impatient listening to an explanation.

Auditory learners prefer listening to explanations over reading them and may like to study by reciting information aloud. This type of learner may want to have background music while studying, or they may be distracted by noises and need a quiet space to study.

Kinesthetic learners learn by doing and touching. They may have trouble sitting still while studying, and they are better able to understand information by writing it down or doing handson activities.

The Lord has given each individual a different learning style, or bent, when it comes to receiving and processing information. It has been determined by educators that a child normally learns best by using a blend of the different learning styles; however, one learning style is often preferred over the other two. One thing needs to be clear. Learning is not about how smart a person is. Learning is about the bent God has given a person to use as he learns. The Purpose Associates state, "The learning styles theory implies that how much individuals learn has more to do with whether the educational experience is geared toward their particular style of learning than whether or not they are "smart." In fact, educators should not ask, "Is this student smart?" but rather 'How is this student smart?'" Therefore, a child's bent is vital information for parents to discover. Finding out a child's bent is not rocket science, but a science nonetheless. There are numerous methods accessible on the Internet to aid in this endeavor. Take the time to determine your child's learning style so you can properly implement a discipleship strategy. Learning can be made easier and more valuable when your kid's bent is known and the proper learning technique is utilized. Knowing the unique bent of each child in your home can open up a new world of learning and confidence.

When Victor Seribriakoff was fifteen years old, his teacher told him he would never finish school or amount to anything. The teacher also said that he was a "dunce," should drop out of school, and learn a trade. Victor thought long and hard. Eventually, he decided to take his teacher's advice. Over the next seventeen years he went from job to job aimlessly drifting with no purpose to his life. Since his teacher told him he was a "dunce," he acted like one. At the age of thirty-two years old something amazing happened in Victor's life. He was given a test to measure his Intelligent Quotient. The score revealed he was a genius. Victor Seribriakoff had an IQ of 161! As a result, he started acting like a genius. With his newfound confidence, Victor began writing books, became an inventor, and had a successful career in business.

APPENDIX 2
DISCIPLESHIP GROWTH PLAN

What's your strategy?

The Rumble in the Jungle was one of the greatest and memorable boxing matches in Heavyweight Championship history. On October 30, 1974, Muhammad Ali and George Foreman battled in Kinsasha, Zaire. Ali was known as a technical fighter. He could add up points in a match rapidly in any given round with his finesse and quickness. On the other hand, Foreman was known as "the bruiser." He would approach each fight with two things in mind. Hit hard and make the match as short as possible. The two fighters could not be more different. As the first round began, no one was surprised when Ali scored several points with his skill and speed. But Ali had a problem; Forman was unfazed. By the end of the first round Ali knew something had to change. With the sound of the bell to begin round two, Ali came out with a new strategy. Foreman came after Ali and began an onslaught of heavy blows and powerful punches. However, Ali held his arms close to his body for protection. As the second round progressed, Foreman began to tire. At opportune times, Ali would also lay against Foreman forcing him to hold up his weight. This too fatigued Foreman. By the fifth round Foreman was drained. Ali's strategy was working. Ali began to land punches with astonishing accuracy to Foreman's head and face. As the eighth round began, Foreman's strength was gone. His punches were weak and unproductive. Muhammad Ali regained his title by knocking George Foreman out in the eighth round. Later in an interview, Howard Cosell asked Ali about his tactic of leaning on the ropes, covering his body with his arms, and absorbing Foreman's punches. Ali called his new strategy the "Rope-a-dope."

Muhammad Ali's brilliant strategy paid off. He was able to use his body to absorb Foreman's hay-maker blows to eventually tire him out and defeat his much stronger opponent. The right strategy works when properly implemented and executed. Do you have a strategy for discipling your children? Believe it or not, just like Ali and Foreman you are in a rumble in the jungle. Your fight is for your children's time, attention, and eternity. But your fight is not with your kid, not by a long shot. It is with the Devil. He wants nothing more than to steal, kill, and destroy you and all your efforts when it comes to discipling your family. Rest assured if you do not have a strategic plan for discipleship in place for your home, Satan will have no trouble causing mayhem and thwarting your attempts of leading your family.

The Lord has placed in every parent's life a special gift. The Bible says, "Children are a heritage from the Lord, offspring a reward from Him" (Ps. 127:3). With this gift comes responsibility. Parents are given the ominous task of being the primary disciplers of the children in their home. King Solomon gave special instructions to parents when he said, "Train up a child in the way he should go: and when he is old, he will not depart from it" (Prov. 22:6 KJV). As the chief disciplemaker, the Lord expects parents to produce a craving in their children for Him as they mature and get older. When you know your child's learning style, you'll be able to help them grow in their relationship with the Lord. Especially during adolescence, God desires parents to cultivate a solid faith foundation in their children. Having a solid foundation will give them the ability to have a long and prosperous life that will be pleasing to the Lord.

To make this foundation solid, it's important to focus on five important aspects of discipleship. Parents have the chance to firmly plant in their kids' lives the desire to know God's Word, to live lives of prayer, to practice spiritual disciplines, to share their faith, and to serve others. Simply put, parents get to teach their children to love God and love others. One way to create a solid foundation is for parents to utilize a biblical tool called "The Discipleship Growth Guide (DG^2)." You'll be able to utilize this tool to assist in guiding your child's spiritual growth in these five areas. The DG^2 is not a discipleship program or Bible study; rather, it is a way the discipler can biblically direct the overall process in the disciple-making effort.

Parents will be able to cultivate these five areas in their children's lives when they sit together, when they walk together, when they go to bed, and when they get up in the morning. While parents spend time with their children, they intentionally make these five areas a natural part of their conversations. As primary disciplers, you'll encourage your kids in these five important aspects to ensure proper spiritual growth. The five areas are:

Bible Reading

Daily Bible reading – A disciple needs to read God's Word every day. The goal is not to get through the Bible but let the Bible get through you. The Bible says, "As I opened my mouth, He gave me the scroll to eat, saying, "Son of man, eat this book that I am giving you. Make a full meal of it!" So I ate it. It tasted so good—just like honey" (Ezek. 3:2 MSG).

Yearly systematic Bible reading – God's Word should be comprehended as a whole not just in part. The Bible says, "Do your best to present yourself to God as one approved, a worker who does not need to be ashamed and who correctly handles the Word of truth" (2 Tim. 2:15).

Scriptural processing – God desires His disciples to not just read the Word but to live it out. The Bible says, "Do not merely listen to the Word, and so deceive yourselves. Do what it says" (Jas. 1:22).

Prayer Time

Daily prayer time – A disciple needs to set aside time during each day to have a conversation with God. The Bible says, "Then Jesus told His disciples a parable to show them that they should always pray and not give up" (Lk. 18:1).

Prayer focus – A disciple should pray with adoration. The Bible says, "Our Father in heaven, hallowed be your name" (Mt. 6:9). A disciple needs to pray and ask for forgiveness. The Bible says, "If we confess our sins, He is faithful and just and will forgive us our sins and purify us from all unrighteousness" (1 Jn. 1:9). A disciple should pray with thanksgiving. The Bible says, "Give thanks to the Lord, for He is good; His love endures forever" (1 Chr. 16:34). A disciple needs to pray for his or her needs. The Bible says, "Give us today our daily bread" (Mt. 6:11). A disciple should pray for others. The Bible says, "pray for each other so that you may be healed" (Jas. 5:16b).

Prayer application – God longs for you to spend significant and quality time with Him. The Bible says, "Let us draw near to God with a sincere heart and with the full assurance that faith brings" (Heb. 10:22).

Spiritual Disciplines
Scripture memorization – A disciple should put God's Word in his or her memory. As a general rule, a person should have at least two verses of Scripture memorized for every year they have been a follower of Christ. The Bible says, "I have hidden your Word in my heart that I might not sin against you" (Ps. 119:11).

Tithing – Believers are commanded to give back to the Lord. You are never more like God than when you give.

Giving to your local church a percentage of what He has allowed you to receive is important. It is not about how much a person gives; rather, it is about how much he keeps. The Bible says, "Bring the whole tithe into the storehouse" (Mal. 3:10).

Fasting – Fasting occasionally from entertainment, the Internet, food, or other things helps keep life in perspective. Fasting provides an opportunity to set aside distractions and focus solely on God. The Bible says, "But when you fast, put oil on your head and wash your face, so that it will not be obvious to others that you are fasting, but only to your Father, who is unseen; and your Father, who sees what is done in secret, will reward you" (Mt. 6:17-18).

Witnessing
Pray for the lost – Witnessing begins by praying for the lost. Disciples should be praying specifically for people who do not know the Lord. The Bible says, "Brothers and sisters, my heart's desire and prayer to God for the Israelites is that they may be saved" (Rom. 10:1). Paul's word for prayer literally means to beg. Disciples should beg God for the salvation of their friends, family, and others.

Prepare to lead others – Disciples need to learn how to lead others to Christ. The Bible says, "Always be prepared to give an answer to everyone who asks you to give the reason for the hope that you have" (1 Pet. 3:15).

Talk about God – God expects the disciple to share the good news of the gospel. Disciples can regularly talk about God in their conversations and invite people to discuss spiritual matters. The Bible says, "Go into all the world and preach the gospel to all creation" (Mk. 16:15).

Ministry

Discover their gifts – Disciples need to discover the gifts God has given them. The Bible says, "We have different gifts, according to the grace given to each of us. If your gift is prophesying, then prophesy in accordance with your faith" (Rom. 12:6).

Use their gifts – God has entrusted believers with gifts to serve others. Gifts are not designed to be hidden or to be used selfishly. The Bible says, "Each of you should use whatever gift you have received to serve others" (1 Pet. 4:10).

Focus on love – God has given believers gifts to serve others in love. The Bible says, "Now eagerly desire the greater gifts. And yet I will show you the most excellent way" (1 Cor. 12:31).

Keep in mind that the real goal of discipleship is to become more like Jesus. Discipleship is not something that can be rushed; it is a lifelong process. Take your time. Concentrate on one or two parts of the DG^2 at a time. Remember the elephant illustration from the Day 10 reading? Don't overdo it. Add more elements when you feel your kids are ready. DG^2 is a starting point that gives parents what they need to provide the fundamentals to promote genuine spiritual growth. DG^2 can help you lead your children to pursue Christ daily, be transformed in Christ completely, and surrender to Christ ultimately. When you use some or all of these five important areas in your discipleship efforts, you can confidently know your kids will have a solid foundation as a disciple now and "not depart from it" (Prov. 22:6b KJV) when they get older.

Dr. John Geddie went to Aneityum in 1848 as a missionary. Aneityum is the southernmost island of Vanuatu off the eastern coast of Australia. He had a vision to reach the Aneityum people for Christ. He worked hard sharing the Gospel for twenty-four years. Today, a stone tablet, placed in his honor, is inscribed with these words: When he landed, in 1848, there were no Christians. When he left, in 1872, there were no heathen.

It took patience, faithfulness, perseverance, dedication, and focus to accomplish his goal of reaching the people of Aneityum with the truth of the Gospel. He made a difference, but it took time. Will you be willing to do the same to achieve your goals in discipling your kids?

Do you know how to get things done?

When Abby and Adam were little, my wife and I would occasionally get treated to a dance fest extravaganza. Our daughter Abby, who was about five at the time, would dress up in her leotard and dance with elegance across the floor while music played softly in the background as we sat in amazement. She would mesmerize her mom and me with her fluid motion and dazzling artistry. Abby, however, was never one to leave her little brother out of the family entertainment. Adam, who was two, would also get into the act. His sister had him join in the presentation as her partner but dressed in a pink tutu. He would come running through the den more like a linebacker than a ballerina. Together they would jump, twirl, and spin across their stage and right into our hearts. By the end of their performance, their mother and I would cheer with laughter and delight. Those were times we'll never forget.

For the longest time I could not figure out how Abby was able to get her brother into that pink tutu so easily. Then it dawned on me. Adam had always been a big ham and loved to have people laugh at him. He enjoyed being the center of attention. Abby understood him and knew how to use it to her advantage. She was a master at getting things done and still is.

How are you at getting things done? Let's take the last few days of reading and put them all together. Now that you understand your child's learning style and know what the Discipleship Growth Guide (DG^2) is all about, we can combine the two. Hopefully through today's reading you'll be able to come up with a strategy to help your children grow into solid disciples of Christ. But you have to remember one very important thing. Be selective and don't get overwhelmed with all these ideas. Your job as your child's discipler is for the long haul so take into account that you have to pace yourself!

Visual Bent

For a kid who has a visual bent, parents can easily implement the DG^2 strategy. A visual learner likes to use pictures, maps, charts, and other visual aids to learn about God and His Word. Also, a child that has a bent toward a visual learning style needs to be able to see the actual passage in the Bible. They have the tendency to remember where certain verses are located on a page. Parents can encourage their kids to set aside time each day to get alone with their Bible and read it for themselves. In addition, parents can recommend that they keep a prayer journal of how God is working in their lives. Memorizing Scripture and learning an evangelistic presentation are not difficult for visually bent kids. These attributes can easily be processed in conversations with children when parents "sit at home and when you walk along the road, when you lie down and when you get up" (Deut. 6:7).

Bible Reading – Children with a visual bent like pictures. Parents can encourage their kids to picture biblical scenes in their minds and imagine what they could have looked like. Parents can help their children visualize the people, the things they were doing, and the items they were using. This will help kids experience the scene in their minds and promote proper learning of the Bible. This process can be used with almost every passage in Scripture. Parents should promote the use of highlighters and note taking when their child studies. It is also important for kids to go to a quiet place when they read the Bible.

Prayer Time – Children with a visual bent are usually organized and like to see things to learn.

Parents can encourage their kids to write out their prayers or prayer list. They could prompt them to categorize their lists into logical sections to help them organize their thoughts. As they pray daily, parents should encourage their children to visualize the people and places they have listed. This will help them to connect their hearts to their lists.

Spiritual Disciplines – A child with a visual bent will excel at Scripture memorization. Visual people tend to picture words and remember them well. Parents can have their children write verses on cards and regularly look at them for memorizing purposes. Parents should encourage their kids to break down verses into sections. As they learn each part, they will be able to memorize the verse more easily. If a child does not have an income, parents can let them be the one who puts the offering into the church. If they are employed, parents should encourage them to tithe. Whichever the case, parents should make sure to talk about and show their child the things inside and outside the church the money goes to support. This will help them visualize where the money goes and what it is used for. Parents should also encourage their children to read the verses regarding tithing and fasting. This will help them better understand the importance of these disciplines.

Witnessing – There are a number of witnessing methods and plans of salvation children can learn. Parents can have their kids memorize several of these ways of leading people to Christ.

Then parents should help their children imagine witnessing situations and help them role-play encounters. As God gives them the opportunity to share the gospel, kids will be more confident and better prepared.

Ministry – Children who are visually bent thrive in a ministry atmosphere where they can be on the front end of the planning stages of events or activities. Parents should encourage their kids to use their gifts to help with planning or organizing.

Auditory Bent
For children who are more geared with an auditory bent, parents can easily apply the DG^2 strategy. Because these children excel when they can process theology by talking it out, parents need to create an atmosphere in the home that welcomes open discussion. Parents should encourage their kids to participate in Bible study and prayer groups, memorize Scripture, listen to Christian music, and subscribe to podcasts of their favorite Bible teachers. Afterwards, parents can

help their children process their discoveries when they "sit at home and when you walk along the road, when you lie down and when you get up" (Deut. 6:7). Kids with an auditory bent make excellent evangelists and servants in ministries.

Bible Reading – Auditory children learn best when they hear information verbally, even if it is their own voice. Parents can have their kids read the Bible out loud daily and listen to podcast sermons or an audio Bible regularly. Each day, parents should set aside time to have discussions with their children on what they are reading. Auditory learners are typically talkative and enjoy discussions to process what they are studying. Parents need to encourage lots of questions from their disciples.

Prayer Time – Children with an auditory bent love to hear their own voice. Parents should encourage their kids to daily pray out loud or sing their prayer to God. At home, parents can have their children pray aloud before a meal and at bedtime. This helps give them confidence when they have opportunities to pray in public. Parents should also encourage their children to make it a habit to verbally praise God, confess their sin, give thanks to the Lord, and personally pray for others. Each day, parents should set aside time to have discussions with their children on what they are praying about to help them process what's going on in their life.

Spiritual Disciplines – A child with an auditory bent is proficient when it comes to memorizing Scripture. Auditory learners do well with memorization when they say a verse out loud or put it to music. Singing Scripture usually comes easily to an auditory learner. This type of learner can excel when he or she uses repetition to memorize. Parents should also teach their auditory learners about other spiritual disciplines such as tithing and fasting. A parent can read and discuss with them passages from the Bible that teach the importance of these subjects.

Witnessing – Auditory children can present the gospel well because of their good oratory skills. When equipped with an easy to remember gospel presentation, an auditory child can be used by God to share the plan of salvation effectively. Parents need to help their kids practice presenting the gospel to give them confidence and make them more proficient.

Ministry – Children who have an auditory bent thrive in ministries that allow them to use their speaking ability. They can be used in a variety of public speaking opportunities inside and outside the church. Parents may need to coach their children through any stage fright they may experience; however, it's worth the effort in the long run. Parents can also encourage their children to volunteer at organizations as greeters, receptionists, and tour guides.

Kinesthetic Bent
Parents with children who have a bent toward kinesthetic learning have their work cut out for them. Fortunately, experts from ldpride.net indicate that only a

small portion of individuals have this learning style as their primary bent. However, there are some helpful ways to make implementing the DG^2 strategy possible. As the primary disciplers, parents can utilize skits, object lessons, and movies to help their students know more about God and His Word. Trips to religious sites or institutions also help in their learning experience. Parents can solidify their child's knowledge by using beats or clapping rhythms to help clarify information and memorize Scripture. The key is making it hands on. It is important that children with a kinesthetic bent be active in evangelism and ministries in their church. As a result, parents can help their kids process their experiences when they "sit at home and when you walk along the road, when you lie down and when you get up" (Deut. 6:7).

Bible Reading – Children with a kinesthetic bent like experiential activities. Parents should try to create an atmosphere that allows hands on discovery of the Scripture. Parents can use objects and props to teach their kids and help them relate to the Bible. Having children act out a story as a parent reads aloud helps them understand the passage on a deeper level. These techniques can be applied in practically every part of Scripture. Parents can also promote the use of highlighters and note taking when their children study the Bible. Parents should be aware that children with a kinesthetic bent need to take frequent breaks when they read their Bible because they often have short attention spans and can easily become distracted.

Prayer Time – Kids with a kinesthetic bent are usually good at imitation. Parents should let their children hear them pray and give them opportunities to pray along with them. Since kinesthetic children have a hard time sitting still, they should change positions frequently or move around when they pray. Parents can help their kids pray more specifically by encouraging them to hold a picture of the people or places they are praying for. Also, prayer walking is a natural activity for children who have a kinesthetic bent.

Spiritual Disciplines – A child with a kinesthetic bent can excel at Scripture memorization as long as he or she is able to be physically active. Parents should encourage these children to use hand motions and props when memorizing verses. Also, activities such as fiddling with objects or being in an unconventional position helps these kids focus. Parents need to be aware that kinesthetic children need frequent breaks when memorizing Scripture. This will reduce their tendency to become distracted. Parents should also allow their kids to give an offering each week at church. Afterwards, parents can to talk to them about the privilege of giving and the reasons why believers give to the church.

Witnessing – Because kinesthetically-bent children are usually good imitators, they can do well with evangelism when they are able to watch a demonstration. Parents need to consider taking their kids witnessing as many times as possible either with the church or as a family. Parents should also take their children on mission trips whenever feasible.

Ministry – Kids who are kinesthetically-bent love to act things out and be physical. It's important that parents encourage their kids to use their gifts in the community and in the church. Parents need to involve their children in the church's drama or creative arts ministries. They can be of great benefit to a church because they tend to gravitate toward expressing themselves through acting things out.